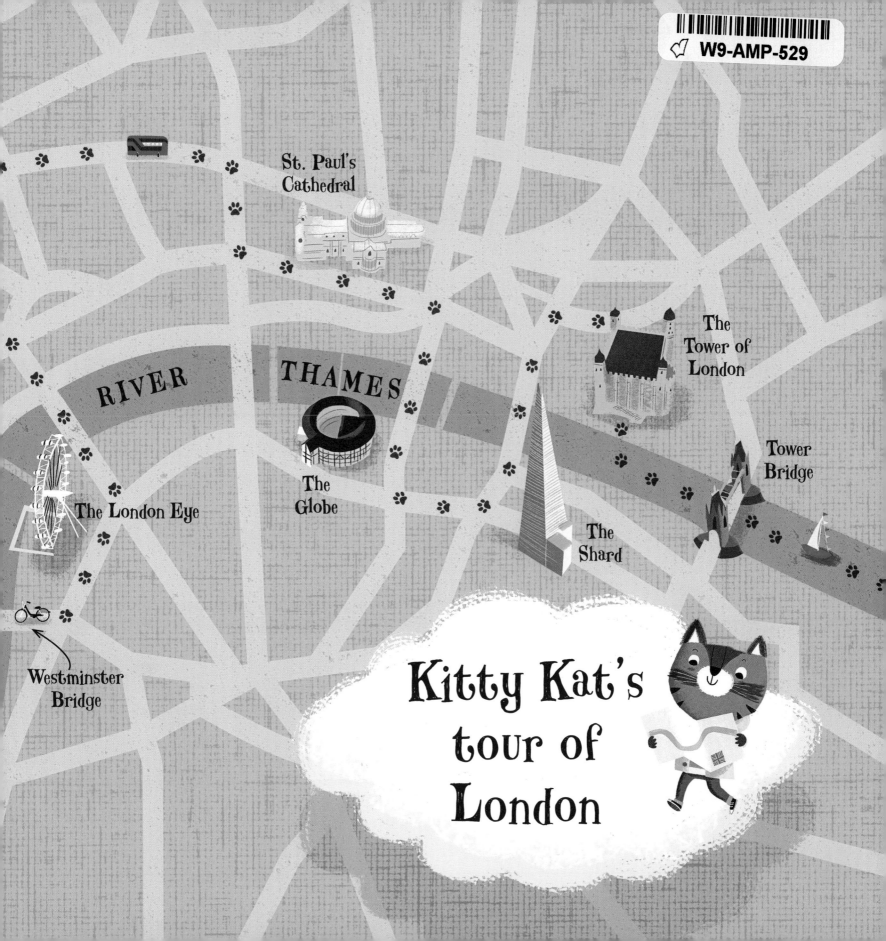

St. Paul's Cathedral

RIVER THAMES

The Tower of London

Tower Bridge

The London Eye

The Globe

The Shard

Westminster Bridge

Kitty Kat's tour of London

Kitty Kat, Kitty Kat, where have you been?

I've been to London, to visit the Queen.

Russell Punter

Illustrated by Dan Taylor

Kitty Kat, Kitty Kat,
where have you been?

I've been to London
to visit the Queen.

Kitty Kat, Kitty Kat,
what did you see?

I'll tell you the story,
just listen to me...

I sailed up the Thames,
where a chilly wind blew.

They raised Tower Bridge so that I could get through.

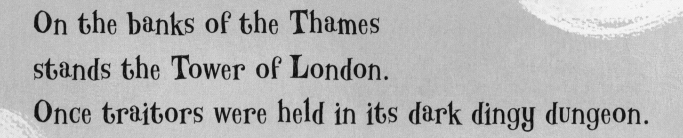

On the banks of the Thames
stands the Tower of London.
Once traitors were held in its dark dingy dungeon.

I met the Beefeaters, who work there today.
They guard the Crown Jewels – it's a sparkling display.

The Shard is a tower
with a breathtaking view.

I took in the sights
from floor seventy-two.

I strolled to the Globe
where I stood in the yard,
for a play by Will Shakespeare. Some call him the Bard.

At Saint Paul's Cathedral,
I had fun with sound.

In the dome, if you whisper...

you're heard all around.

If you don't want to walk,
you can hop on a bus.

One whizzed me through London without any fuss.

In Trafalgar Square,
where tourists rush by,
a statue of Nelson looks down from on high.

He fought in sea battles
a long time ago.
Four mighty bronze lions sit proudly below.

The next thing to try
was the huge London Eye.

It's a wheel that can take you
far up to the sky.

You stand in a capsule.
The wheel turns around.

You can see the whole city,
spread out on the ground.

On Westminster Bridge,
I went for a ride,
to the Houses of Parliament on the far side.

Big Ben is a bell.
It chimes on the hour,
from the belfry inside the Elizabeth Tower.

At Westminster Abbey,
they crown kings and queens.

Close your eyes and imagine
those magical scenes.

I took a black cab
to the Royal Albert Hall,

where a wild-haired conductor
was having a ball.

At Buckingham Palace
the guardsmen marched past.
I'd saved the best part of my journey 'til last.

The Queen's Guard paraded.
Their band played with pride.
When the marching had finished, I strode on inside.

I saw royal paintings...

...the grand dining room.

I was sure I would talk to Her Majesty soon.

When I got to the place
where she sits on the throne,
I was shocked to discover... she wasn't at home!

What a pity, dear Kitty,
You went all that way...

But London is fun,
so I had a great day.

Edited by Lesley Sims

First published in 2015 by Usborne Publishing Ltd., Usborne House, 83-85 Saffron Hill,
London EC1N 8RT, England. www.usborne.com Copyright © 2015 Usborne Publishing Ltd.

The flags of Buckingham Palace

Since 1997, the Union Flag has been flown from the Palace when the Queen is not there. When Her Majesty returns, the Royal Standard is flown.

The Union Flag

The Royal Standard

Nelson's Column

Trafalgar Square

Buckingham Palace

The Royal Albert Hall

Westminster Abbey

The Houses of Parliament